In Search of Zzz's

Being the Wondrous
Journey of the Fool
Finding his Way to Wisdom

In Search of Zzz's

"This is not the Answer,
Or the Name.
It's 'Tongue in Cheek',
A Playful Game."

Author: Numinous Yeca

Cover Art: Francisco Fonsec

Table of Concepts

LE·FOL·

A fool can throw a stone into a pond
that one hundred wise men cannot get out

Saul Bellow

A Fool Awakens to find a Phoenix.

In his fascination, he asks questions, which gains him insights and answers to some of mankind's deepest secrets.

In this wonderfully illustrated book you will discover delight and truth as you make the journey to freedom with the fool.

ZZZs

Have you ever climbed a mountain
from the foothills up?
Can you really reach the horizon
before life fills your cup?

The Phoenix

Far, far away a man cried. A release that quenched his inner fear. He cried for pain, for sorrow, and for joy - he cried that others might receive and gain by giving thought to IS.

Is a thought a thought that thought that all there is, is … IS?

A dream, deep within that curious soul, the soul who thinks it is me - That all of everything within is everything without. And thinking this, I venture out and see all that is, is IN.

ZZZs

Does your journey have an ending
or a beginning with a start?

The Riddle

Sitting down, beneath the canopy of stars I contemplate my riddle. Who can fathom his depths of soul? Who can attain his heights?

An Echo: *I can, for I am he!*

But how, I ask my soul?

In finding peace and giving love and bearing all for all, I free my self.

Soul burns brighter, shedding me for I, until It stands within the fire, a Phoenix from my ashes.

I looked again. I was not wrong; it was me, cleansed of all my wishes.

Do you find that there is meaning to your acts in every part?

Balance

Hail! Oh Fearsome Oracle. Be Phoenix your Name?

"I am your Phoenix, your soul in transit. From your ashes I am free and, if you desire the highest goal, then I am truth from treason.

"For all I say is within you alongside all your doubt, and all you lack, is balance in your imbalance as the scales of your life are lifted higher.

"All is none and none is all there is in perfect unity, for everything unites, one by one, 'til all is one and one is all."

When you see the sun is setting
and you know that night has come;

Truth

Do you tell me of your truth Phoenix? Tell me more, for if this is your truth, I would write it, that it may not perish.

"Poet, who says that truth may perish? It is wrapped in riddle and given you everyday, but you perceive it only to that degree that you are able. For if truth were thrust upon you, then the burden of yourself would be too great, and if truth were taken from you then the burden of the world would be too great.

"For truth is only true to he who sees and untruth is only untrue to he who does not understand the sight. All is truth, for who can disprove nature, and none is truth for who can prove her prophesy. Truth is not discovered nor ever lost, for all truth is is is."

ZZZs

When you find that time is passing
and your work is hardly done;

Prophecy

And the poet in his confusion spoke again and said: Speak to us of prophesy.

"Prophesy, what is prophesy? A prophet is a poet who, reading God's poetry of life, renders it to his fellows with understanding. The poetry of life is the essence of God and is the cornerstone of the earth. Any poet able to understand these words, is a prophet prophesying the beginning of life and the end of the world. For is it not a truth that to live life, the world must end?

"A prophet, in understanding, puts aside the world that he may see clearly and, resurrected, he begins to live."

Can you stop — to look and listen;
find your living in each day?

Desire

The poet smiled and asked again of the Phoenix: What of our desire?

"Desire, oh desire, like black powder burning instantly, it is the purpose of balance. If in your desire, you become unaware of your speed then you are drugged and cannot halt. The persuasion of your desire imbalances your reason and adds fuel to your passion.

"You war continually, within yourself and in the world. To have or to have not, there is your reason, to give or to give not, there is your passion. If you allow desire to be bound by reason then you shut up your life 'till you blow your cool. If you allow desire, to passion sway then you burn up, uncool.

"Therefore do I say, desire, oh desire, it is the purpose of balance."

When you find your peace disturbed,
can you settle in and stay?

Love

Speak to me of Love, oh Phoenix, that I may learn from whence you came.

"Love is all, all is love. Is love? Love is! Love.:The be all to life, the end all to life, the life eternal. Love is the Nature giving of its gifts. Rain for the dry, Sun for the wet, never ending, always beginning. If you meet love, follow, for though his voice is not your own, believe it! For love is to you your reason, your passion and your pain. However strong you grow, love prunes, and however high he takes you, he leads you through the depths. So follow for he gives to them that give and takes from them that take 'til all are returned to his oneness. Feeling love is feeling one with all creation for God's spirit is teaching you your spirit.

"Be not afraid to love, for in all good things is love. How joyous is the waking day, how righteous is the night? How loving is the verdant rain, how thankful is the sun again?

"Contemplate love and cultivate it, let it grow and let it flow. Look on all things in a new day in a new way. Love them of themselves, for are they not God's? Does He not love them all just as they in turn shower the day with their blessing? So must you."

Or, do you race to make up time
to meet a contract always due;

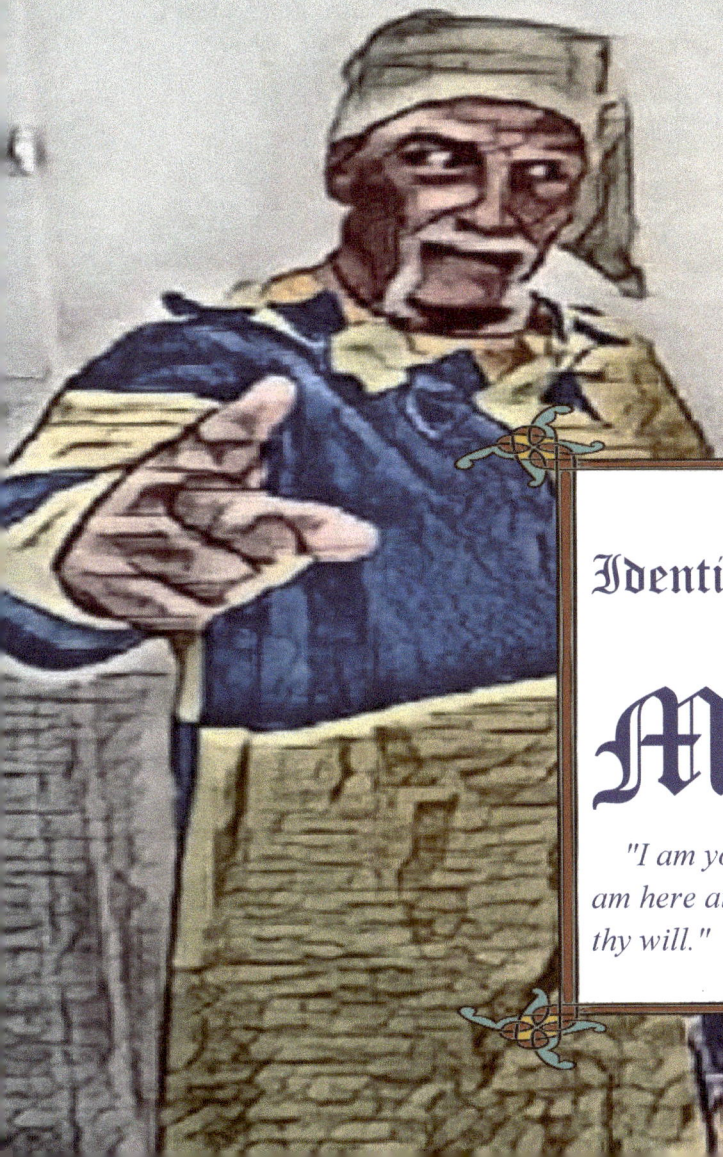

Identity

Master, do not trifle, tell me who you are.

"I am your Phoenix arising from your ashes and I am here at your will. Choose then, for I cannot but do thy will."

Zzz's

Can't you see the progress winning
and that your days alive are few?

Unity

Speak then of unity, marriage of the soul.

"Unity is oneness, divine love in you. It is the flex that phones the thought, the air that's breathed by all living things. United you have always been and united you will always be. Therefore let not your heart be troubled in your lonely nights, for your loneness is only your fear. You are together, let God see you together and fear not, nor despair for you are the one cake. But from individual ears were you baked.

"Let not your love blind you but, rather, let it be a glory to God, set up as an example to the divided. United you know the other's soul is alone as yours is alone, uniting only when, together, you give yourselves to love. And together you live, each separate in their knowledge of God."

ZZZs

There is neither Black nor White,
only spectrum colours seen;

Children

Thinking of desire the poet asked: Speak, Phoenix, of children.

"I am a child and I am old. That which I know of children has been spoken. In my age I look at those who are starting this gift and I am confounded of my speech. There are no children. We are all children.

"What can you know of children? They are never yours, only of you, for they are the inheritors of life and they can never belong to you, for their life is beyond yours. Each one of you thinks your own thoughts, so how then can you impart yours to the children? The child thinks his own for he has never lived your life and you can never live his. You are therefore to be glad for the children and give them love. For they that give love will see loving souls stride out to conquer their own understanding."

And you know nothing of the future
and very little of what has been.

Understanding

And the poet said: What of understanding?

"Listen to my words and I will impart the stuff of life, for is not all life in words as we see it? Understanding is of oneself. It is the perusal of all one knows, bringing to light the realisation that, if one could stop talking and thinking, then there would be no end to one's understanding. For understanding is the instant realisation of a truth, the inspiration that spurs your contemplation. It is the knowing that is the balance between your superstition and your belief.

"Understanding is the giving of Love and the partaking of Wisdom. To understand, one must look deep within and see the universe of universes. If one does understand, then in his wisdom he will give freely and lovingly of all to all."

Zzz's

Have you seen the problems stopped,
and the wars have an end;

Time

The Poet wondered: And of Time?

"I see it is time. I will speak with you of charity and the time. Time is God's charity, a measure of love where we might comprehend the immeasurable love that is our's to give away. Held in time, love speeds, in time, whilst slowing the days; and given freely of love, it slows the time in speeding the days.

"This morning you said ~ Now I will arise to meet the day. This evening you will say ~ Now I will retire to rest 'til day. If past and future can both be Now, then there is no time, for all time is now, and now is the only time you can live.

"If this is so then your time is not your own, but God's who gave it to you so that you would have opportunity to spend it wisely and give of it all you have for in charity He frees you from time. Give therefore all that you have for are we not at one with all in your need of God's bounty. If therefore you are given to, praise God that you have given so you may not be overburdened, but do not burden the giver by not receiving, for you are all transceivers on God's wavelength, partaking of the circle that neither begins nor ends. The zero that ends all and begins all, that encompasses all and is within all, the sight and sound of God."

Zzz's

Or overcoming old evils
bring peace around the bend?

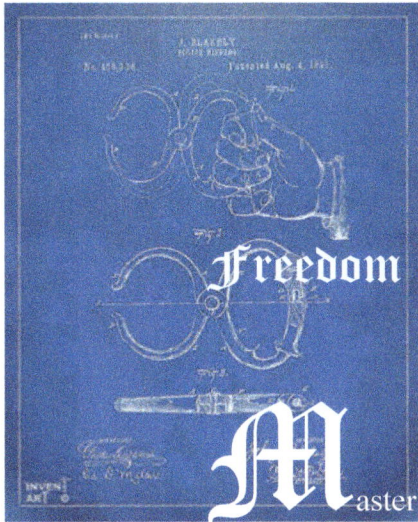

Freedom

Master, have you finished? Will you tell us of Freedom?

"Have I not? Then let me finish. I have seen you revel in your separate individualism. Hear this. No one is individual to the extent of separateness from God. You are like snowflakes in a storm. All are individual patterns, but all are still snow. Crystallise yourselves, by all means, but see how you drift with others of your kind. You are not free, you who feast to freedom. For the bonds on your freedom are the very bonds you have set up for your security. Find your security in God's freedom and the shattered bonds leave you free to bond your greater freedom. Thus ever is man either free or not free, according to his charity. And to be free, for God's charity to give away, you must first have the love that teaches the wisdom of charity.

"In your freedom are many shackles, links to chain you. Your laws and your crimes, your punishment and your joy, your sorrow and your self-knowledge, your teaching and your pain, your friends and your pleasures, your good and your evil, your prayer and your life, your beauty and your death, your religion and your way of life. All these have I spoken of beforetimes and in times to come, for each preys upon the minds of the unprepared.

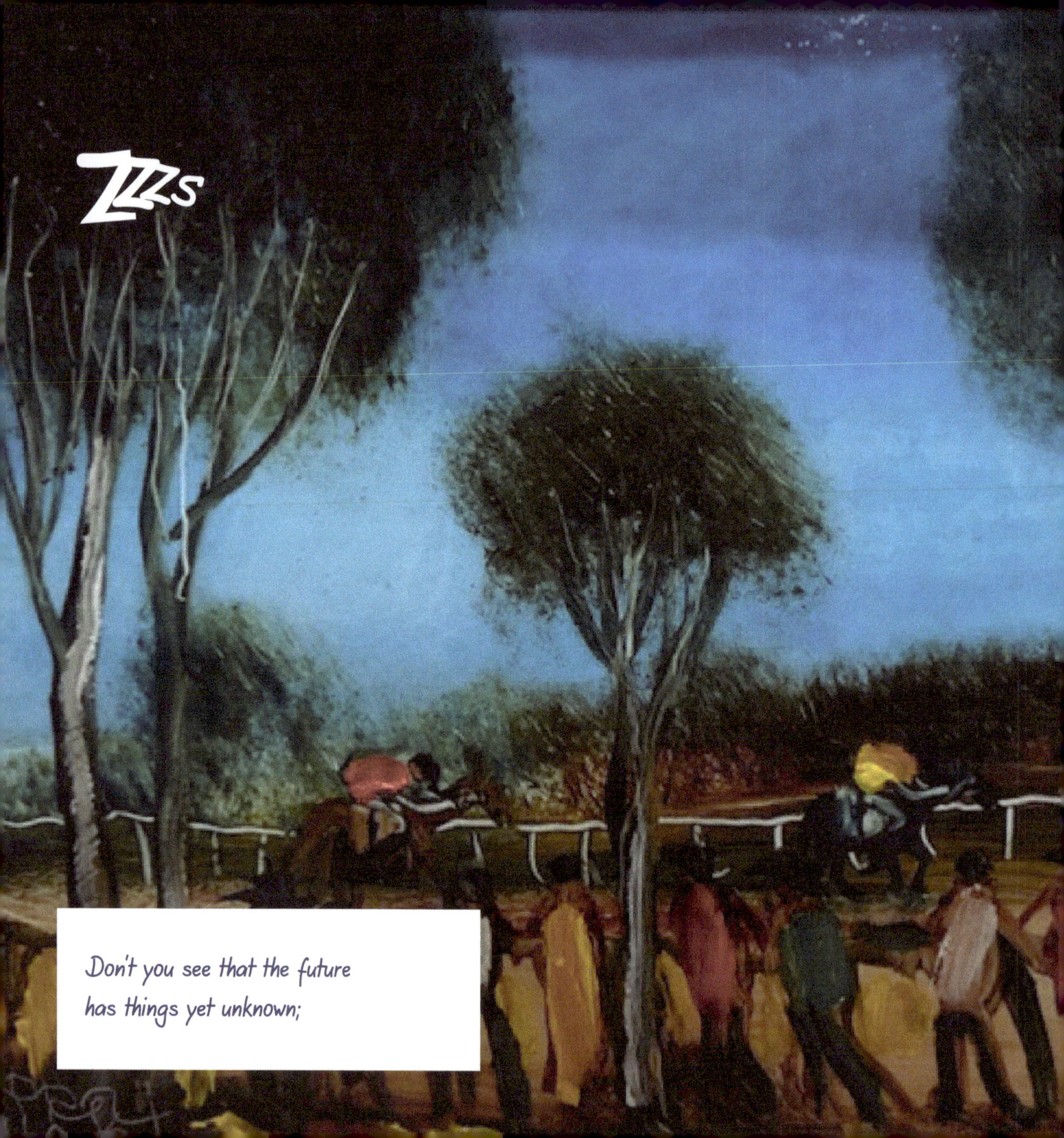

Don't you see that the future
has things yet unknown;

Harmony

Teach me, that I may be at peace and in balance.

"*Teach not, for learning is in the listener. Rather, give of yourself, your understanding, that it may be compared with the thought of the receiver that he may realise some truth. Then I will learn that my teaching is not in vain. Therefore, I say to you that, in stillness and balance is harmony with God, and any choice that we may make is God. Within us in our balance.*

"*Your laws are laid down by your overseers and are laid down for the people to keep or break. They are the weights on a racehorse to keep him equal in opportunity for the laying of odds. These gamblers comprehend the odds are not enough; when all numbers are one and every gamble is a certainty, laws no longer bind you to the racecourse, for you can shed your weights and run free in the sight of heaven.*"

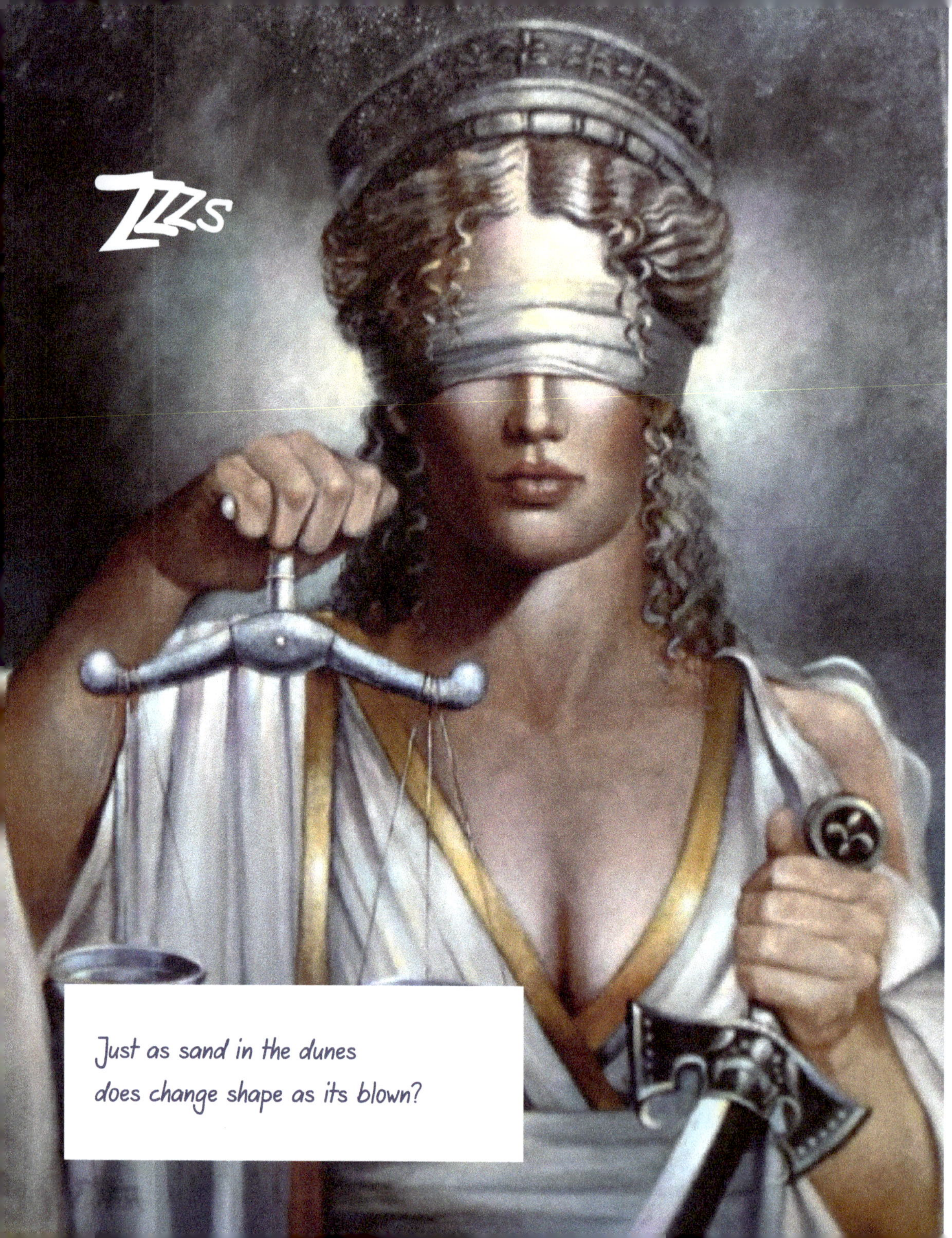

Just as sand in the dunes
does change shape as its blown?

Justice

"Your criminals, in your society, poet: What crime places them outside social recognition? Is it that they, in their haste to be free, have committed some wrong which is harmful to themselves and others? You are mature in your world but still a child and yet, God feeds your spirit that you might live. That man, that criminal, is no stranger, although you share not his knowledge. For as much as he has wronged you, you have allowed it. His knowledge is his, and yours is yours, but all knowledge is one and the wrong is as much the wronged as the wrongdoer. If you commit a wrong, thank God that the punishment is meet - to teach those that follow in the path and also those who went before, who may learn of the trip they missed in their passage.

"Learn therefore, also, that neither the trip nor the passage is the destination and, therefore, judge not. In judging you are putting yourself in a wrong perspective and, knowing not the full extent of your own belief, you may wrong yourself. To serve justice therefore, put all deeds to the light. If they cast no shadow, how can one judge them? And if they do have shadow, then to judge them, one must also be in the world of shadow. Where then is your justice, for who would shackle his soul in the dark?

Zzzs

Are you invincible,
omnipotent, omniscient?

Sorrow and Pain

The poet wept, not knowing why.

"Poet, have you heard? Do you perceive the joy of all things? Then I will speak of sorrow that your joy may be set free. Is joy better than sorrow or is sorrow the better? Listen carefully; do you hear joy's lament, a song to free your soul? Do you perceive in joy your sorrow, a tear for greatness seen? Joy is the fulfilment of the future, as sorrow is the fulfilment of the past. There are some who find joy in everything. There are others who find sorrow. Let your Soul be free in the ecstasy of this moment yet balanced with sorrow. The deaf and blind in their lack seek continuous ecstasy. As great as your charity will you feel your sorrow cutting deep and, in your sorrow, will your joy be the healing of you. For one cannot be healed who has not hurt.

"Speaking, therefore, of pain I ask you, do you feel the pain? It grows daily with your understanding and is the book of all knowledge. Feel it, contain it, for you are but the fruit that holds your seed of knowledge. You have chosen your pain, so choose then your medicine and speak no complaint. For you wrong God if you think that pain is greater than the container. Are your medicines less worthy than their containers? Trust, therefore, and receive pain as much in joy as in sorrow."

Do you find that grass is greener,
or counting chickens pleasant?

Voice of Spirit

"Speak then in your spirit, that Gods oneness may speak through you. Many talk to hear their voice! In your loneliness and your fear, while you listen to the talkers you need not be alone with yourself.

"You clothe your body to escape the eyes of the foul-minded. Yet, are not these modest clothes a facade raised to keep you from yourself? Why do you clothe your days with listening and talking? Speak, and hear the truth your soul desires.

"Do you live in a house or in the blessing of God? Your house is your comfort or your outer temple, shackling you to lustful desires or standing out as your abode in freedom. The house that haunts your will with comfort is a thief that would take your feet from the the earth and your head from the clouds. It would weaken your spirit and resolve, behind it's small doors and shallow windows.

"Your house and clothes and any other possession is yours in your glory to show the wisdom of nothing; Only with non-attachment to this world may you be at peace within."

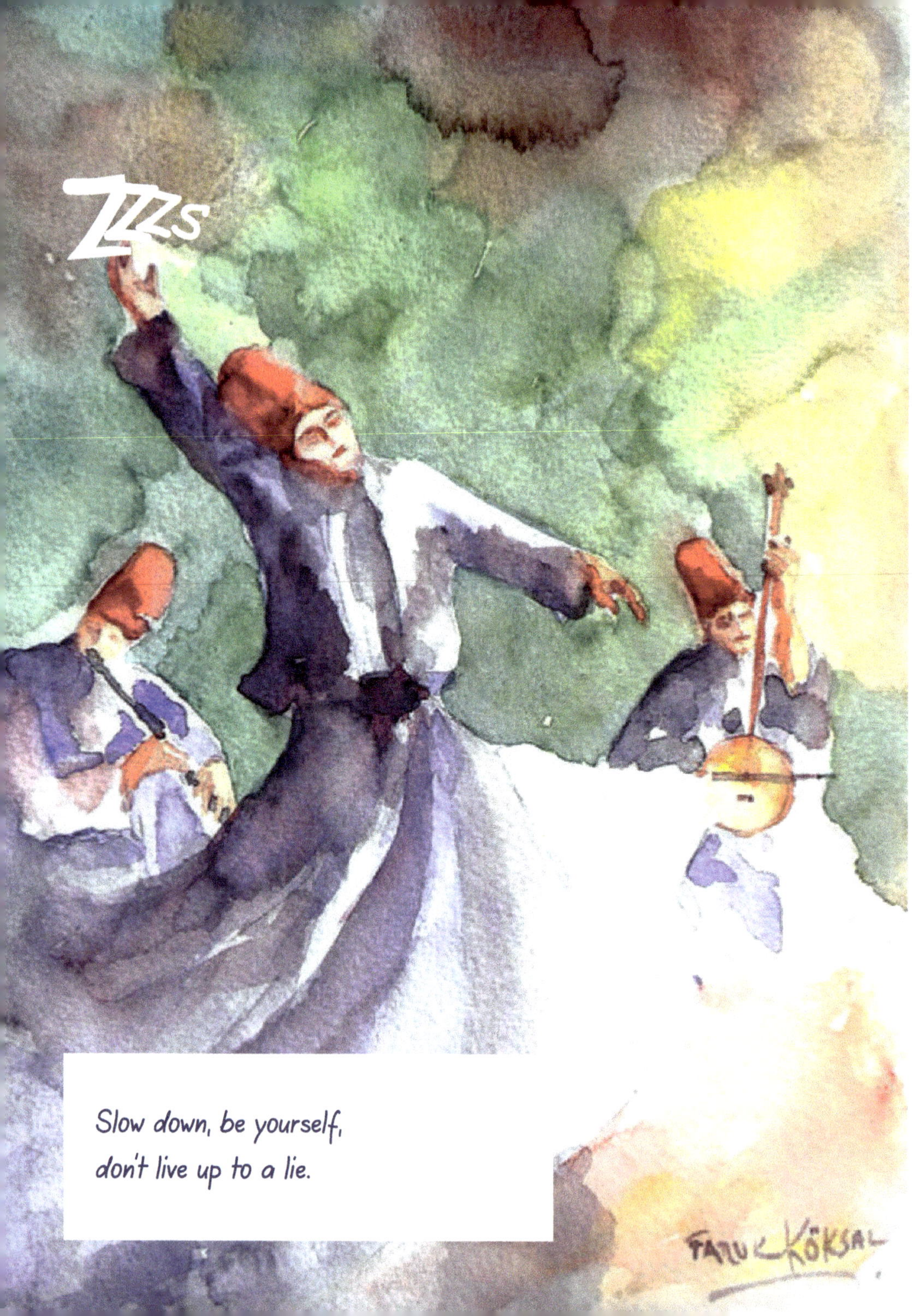

Slow down, be yourself,
don't live up to a lie.

The Eternal Prayer

"This is your Eternal Prayer: that you may be at peace with God and your own soul. For what is Prayer? It is not the anxious seeking of need, but the communion of your spirit with all who pray. You cannot find a supermarket in the street of temples, so ask not what you can receive but ask what it is you can give! In communion with the oneness of God, your prayer is worship in that you desire that which God desires through you. And you give that which God gives through you. And you receive that which God receives through you: For you are but a channel that needs Gods balance.

"Do not distress yourself, therefore, I say. For does not God know your needs? It is his pleasure to fulfil them. If life is a tree, then God blossoms on the tree to fulfil life's need for fragrance, beauty and fruit to beget life. Does he not do this in your life? Think not that God should give to you alone, for that is not balanced. Balance, in your receipt of pleasure you give God pleasure, for you are His blossoms - Here for a season, to give freely of your fragrance, beauty and fruit."

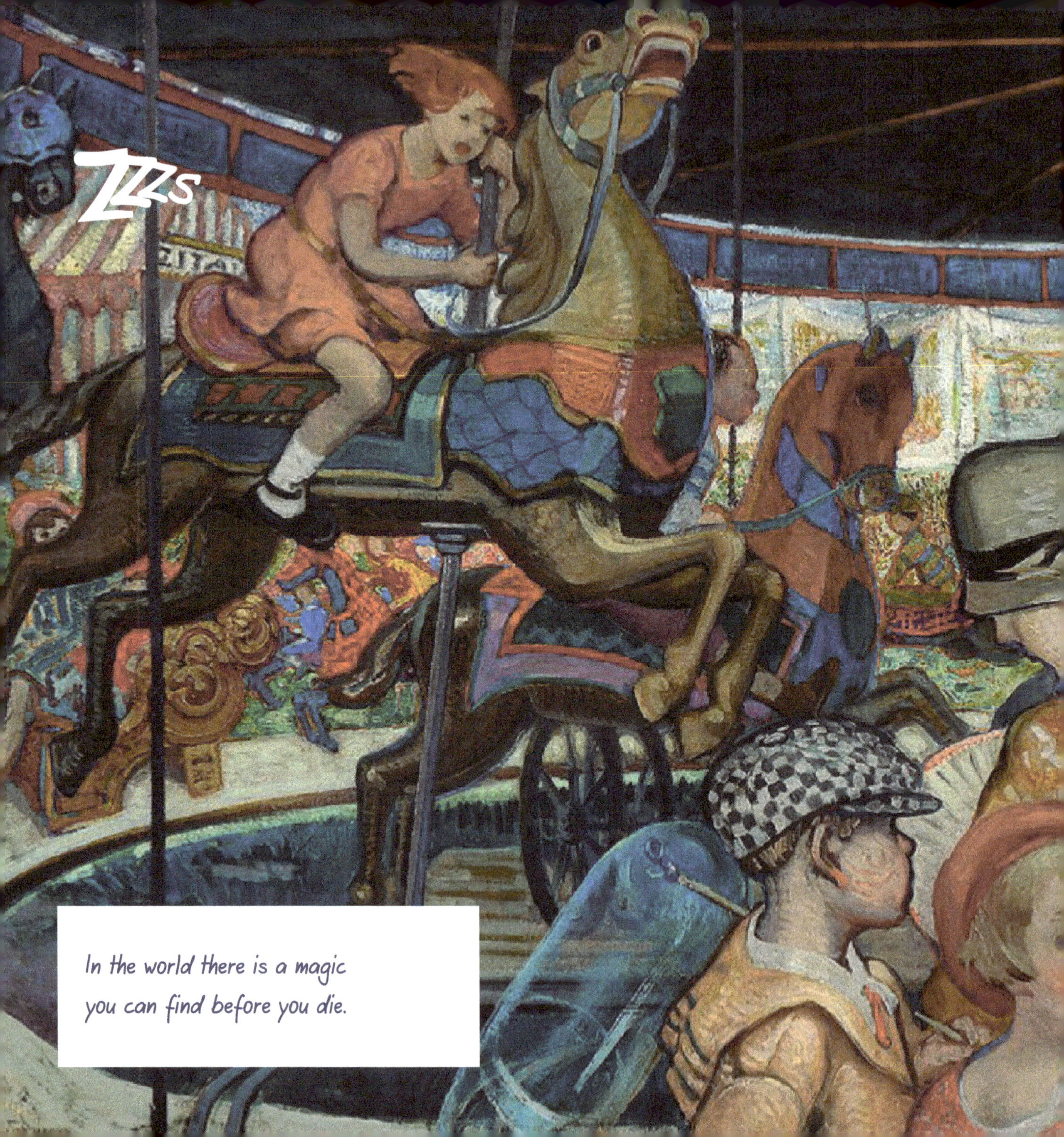

In the world there is a magic
you can find before you die.

Needs

"Listen poet, and I will tell you of your needs. They are the companionship of men, for all men have need to belong. In their need they meet people to seek truth of them. In your acquaintances, meet your need, and in your friends your fulfilment. Your friend is with you in joining or parting, he is the depth to your understanding and the companion with whom you live. Your friendship is the stripping of mystery from Gods love and, in the joy of new-born understanding, your pleasures are shared that each may laugh with God at the beauty of it all.

"Seek not the fulfilment of your needs in the world, but rather in those who can show you beauty, for they are your friends, and the richness of your life. As you give them love so will you be thankful, for they inflame your heart and cast their spell over your soul.

ZZZs

All your anxious doubts and worry
will not take you very far.

Beauty

*"Beauty, in itself, is not your need but your fulfilment.
It is your ecstasy and your life, for if beauty shows
herself to you then have you seen life. Beauty is the
mirror your friends carry to show you to yourself. This is
your religion poet, that your daily prayer fills your
temple and that you give all you have to all there is.*

"Your temple is the moment and all charity is there."

Zzzs

All you have to do is realize,
where you're going, is where you are.

Curiosity

Is that all Phoenix? Have you finished?

"You are curious beyond measure, poet. What would you have me say? A last word, how can I finish? Words are eternal."

Tell me of myself that I may beware.

"Poet, have you been listening? I said: I am your Phoenix, your Soul in transit. Therefore, be not afraid for I am always within, to rise whenever you burn. Death is no terminus. I am with you in your living and your dying for I am the resurrection of your desire to be one with God. I am your soul and I am free.

"You are cautious - you wish to beware? Of whom, of what? Your awareness is tuned in to Gods wavelength for you seek the ISness of yourself. Take any thought you may have and render it to the balance. Take any sentence, reduce it of its negative thought and that which is left is yourself. So, Poet, if you must beware, beware of yourself, for in ego and vanity is your fall

"Here I will say farewell that you may contemplate. Remember; I am only you to me, and you are only me to you."

Zzzs

Have you ever climbed a mountain
from the foothills up?

The Dream

Hail oh fearsome oracle, be Phoenix your name!

For thought I thought was thought indeed if all that is is IS. Did dreamer dream a dream of dreams, does soul sleep deep within? Or do we contain a spark of God within all of without therein? Can we sit down and fathom height or reach attainment in our depths? Are we the fire or the desire, the ashes or the rash wishes? What can I say but what's been said, I've lived and I've been dead? What do you find, within? Your mind, or maybe understanding?

The spark that lit inspirations wick, your Soul, your grasp of NOW. As your candle flame burns higher, remember your beginning, so that when the awesome light gets nigher, know that in NOW, you're living.

And, as my tears did close my eyes, I remembered my notes and I wrote down his last saying.

"I am only you to me, and you are only me to you."

Can you really reach the horizon
before life fills your cup?

Good and Evil

"I have spoken to you of Joy and Sorrow, now hear of Good and Evil. Evil is neither good nor not good. Evil is of your own making. It is not 'not' good, but an illusion of both good and not so good. For if Good were aware of it's own goodness then too would it be aware of latent Evil. Good is but a stream that, either fast, or slow, reaches out to it's beginning in the ocean.

"Evil, therefore, is that within you which would have you drown before seeing Gods ocean of love.

"Learn then that, in all you do, is the latent evil that would have you stop before you reach your goal. You may travel a not so good path or linger, or rest in the shade, or loiter by the fruit-trees, but do not fall into despair or fear! Within you is contained all knowledge: but measure it not, for your container is small and holds only your understanding. And rather than say, 'I have truth' say, 'I have a measure of truth'. Rather then say, 'My path is good' say, "There is a measure of good in my path'. There is Good in all and your self-knowledge is yours, so let not your latent evil spread amongst your contemporaries from your thought or speech, but rather that which is Good."

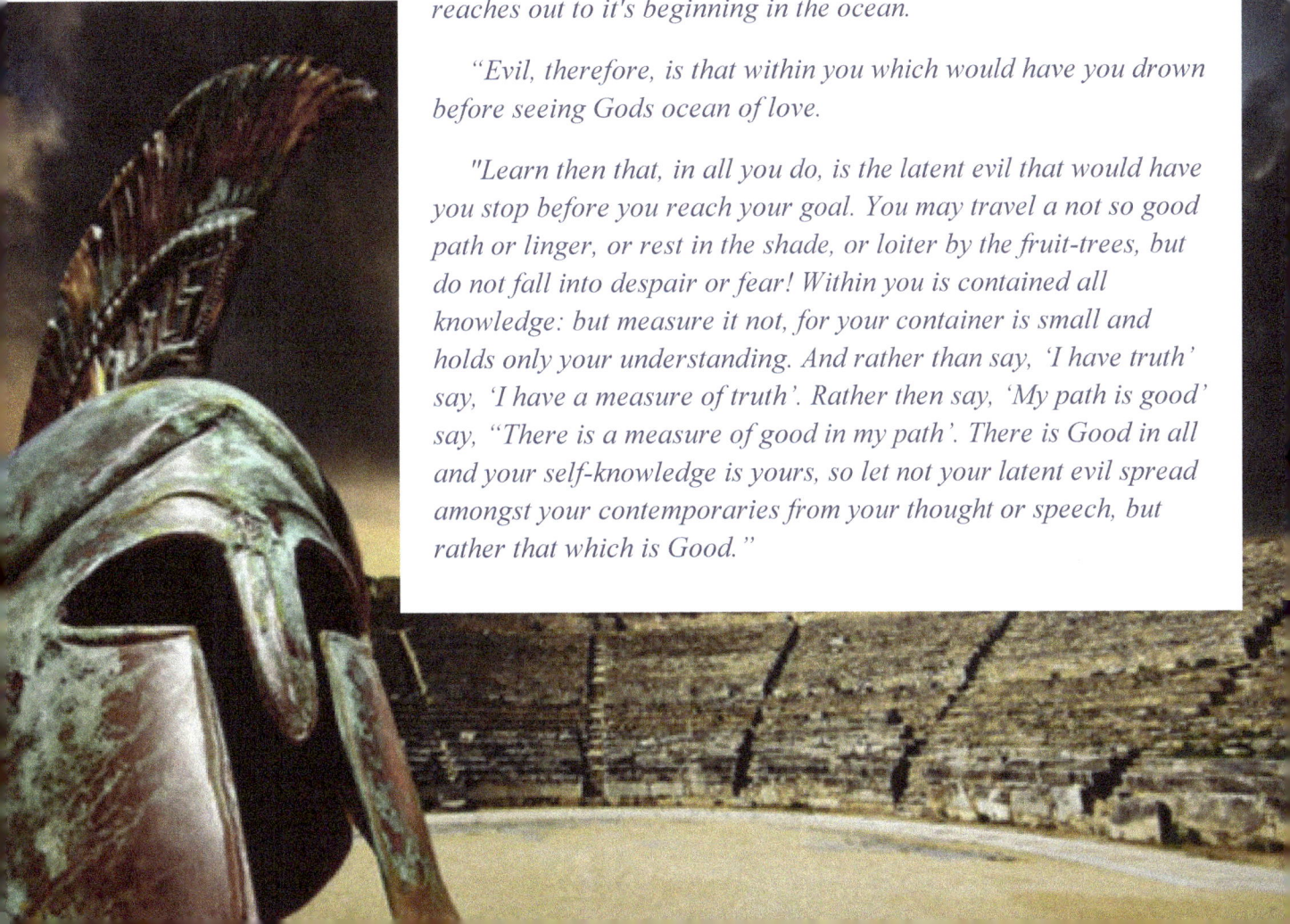

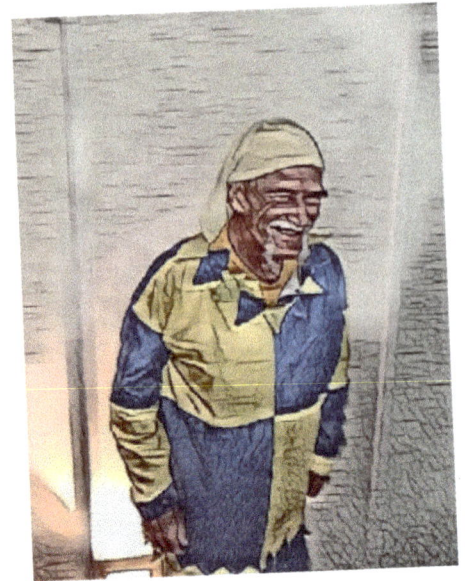

In Search of Zzz's
COPYRIGHT 2021 NUMINOUS YECAM

ISBN: 978-0-6484277-6-6

Copyright 2021 NUMINOUS YECAM
Publisher: Ladder to the Moon Productions
Email: qrcaustralia@gmail.com
Web: laddertothemoon.com.au

About the Author

Numinous Yecam was raised in a British Naval family, schooled by the RN, later he moved to Australia, joined the army, and was trained by RAR. He spent seventeen years outback with a Kadaicha man (Aboriginal shaman) who took him on several walkabouts, showing the author the practices of Dreamtime, finding food and water, and otherwise working on the land in planting and harvesting crops from various Australian terrains. When he retired from truck driving he moved to Brisbane (Australia) and surrounds, where he currently resides.

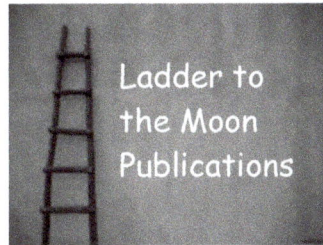

Ladder to
the Moon
Publications

www.laddertothemoon.com.au

Aiming for the Stars is much easier if we stop off at the Moon. We are then out of the atmosphere of our past, and can see things more clearly. We are lighter, can jump higher and further than ever before, and it takes far less energy to start each journey.

The hard part is climbing that Ladder to the Moon.

Acknowledgements:

Most grateful appreciation to Dayal.

To my mother, Fay, who taught me reading and charm, and my father, Ted, who instructed me in discipline.

My siblings, Nicholas, Ian and Meredeth for keeping me keeping on, along with my adoptive mob;

Old Nik, Lyn, Danny, Donny, and Cynthia.

Phoenix Masque by Tom and Cea

Costume by Erin Miller

Praise for the patience of my publisher, Michael Wallace.

And last but not least those friends who have believed in me and made this possible; Cecilia, Raven, Sian and Kristine.

Numinous Yecam.

I am I said because I said I am

my power I know because I know my power

Who it is I am, you may not know

nor how I know you know I know

But how I know is secret self

a secret grown within myself

And if you wish for me to reveal

and have no wish from me to steal

That secret centred in the dawn

that perpetual motion, a spiral born

Then torture self with seeking ways

hunger and thirst for many days

and when at last you search the dark

and find your food in rotten bark

and also slake your thirst in hell

by drinking water from your wishing well

perhaps you'll note the time stand still

and see in life, the power of will.

In Search of Zzz's

Numinous Yecam

www.ingramcontent.com/pod-product-compliance
Lightning Source LLC
Chambersburg PA
CBHW060802150426
42813CB00059B/2848